The Evidence – for Kids

Graphic design by Joe Potter (www.joepotter.com)
Illustrations by Richard Gunther (www.mightymag.org.nz)
Living Waters Publications
P.O. Box 1172
Bellflower, CA 90706, USA
www.raycomfort.com
(562) 920-8431

ISBN # 9 780882 709826

Dedicated to Julia and Summer Zwayne--two precious gifts from God.

Hi kids!

My name is **Albert Brainstein**. I want to talk to you about some very important things. Here's the first...

How do we know that God exists?

You can't [1] see or touch Him.

Let me show you how you can know for sure:

Here is a famous painting.

How do you know that there was a painter?

...the *painting* is proof that there was a painter. Paintings don't paint themselves.

You don't need to *see* the painter or touch him to know that there was a painter. You can know for sure that there was a painter *because you can see the painting!*

Here is creation.

How do you know that there was a Creator?

...creation is proof that there was a[2] Creator. Creation couldn't happen without a Creator.

You don't need to *see* God or touch Him to know that there was a Creator. You can know for sure that there was a creator *because you can see creation!*

If we admire a wonderful painting, we are really admiring a wonderful painter.

Let's look closely at creation to see how wonderful the Creator is:

Think of the cow. It eats green grass and makes it into white milk. *Now that's amazing.* People can't do that. Then the milk can be made into cheese, butter, ice cream, or yogurt. People are more clever than cows, but we can't do what they can do-- turn green grass into white milk, then into cheese, or butter, ice cream or yogurt. Therefore the cow must have been made by Someone who is much more intelligent than people.

Think of the chicken. It can also do something we don't know how to do. Overnight, it turns wheat (and even worms) into delicious eggs. Therefore Someone more intelligent than people made the chicken.

Think of the banana. It is shaped for your hand. It has a wrapper that unzips. It has a "tab" (like the soda can). It's just the right shape for your mouth. It tastes good. It even curves towards your face to make it easy to eat. It is clear that Someone made the banana especially for people (and monkeys) to eat.

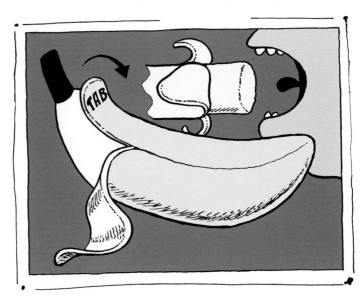

Think of the apple. It too is shaped for your hand. It has a groove for your thumb and one for your forefinger. It tastes good (you can eat the wrapper). It cleans your teeth, and it even has little seeds inside. If you put them into the ground, they make more apples.

Someone made the apple especially for people (and horses) to eat.

Think of the corncob. You can eat it right off the cob. It can be made into corn bread. Or it can even be made into cornflakes and eaten for breakfast.

The banana, the apple and the corncob each grew from the same soil. How does the same soil make them taste so different?

Use your eyes to look into a mirror. Watch them automatically blink--if you can. They are more [3] wonderfully made than any camera anyone has made. Listen to the sounds your ears are catching. See how they are shaped to catch the sound and send it into your brain. Then use your brain to think about your brain. It is *much* more wonderfully created than any computer anyone has made.

Remember, the cleverest scientist can't "make" anything from nothing. He can only use things in God's creation to make [4] other things. But we don't even know how to make a leaf (or even a grain of sand) from nothing.

[1] See John 1:18

[2] See Romans 1:20

[3] See Psalm 94:9

[4] See Hebrews 3:4

[5] See Psalm 19:1-3

[6] See Psalm 14:1

All around us we see the wonders of God's creation showing us how wonderful the ⁵ Creator is. A person who says there is no Creator is not thinking properly. People call someone who doesn't believe in God an "atheist." The Bible calls him a ⁶ "fool."

Let's now look at another important question...

How do we Know That the Bible is True?

The Bible is full of strange and wonderful stories--Jonah and the whale, Daniel in the Lions' den, Jesus walking on water, etc. Could they be stories that people have made up (fairy tales), or did they really happen?

The Bible is actually sixty-six books. Within its pages it says that it was written by people (about 40 of them) and that God helped them do the[1] writing. Here are some good reasons we can know that God helped them:

1. The Bible contains many scientific facts that were written *thousands of years* before people discovered them:

The earth is [2] round.

It floats in [3] space.

Everything is made of [4] invisible things (atoms).

The Scriptures (another name for the Bible) also contain medical facts that were written thousands of years before people discovered them.

Hands must be washed in [5] running water (because of invisible germs). Blood is the source of all [6] life.

The Bible is also full of amazing prophecies (prophecies say what will happen in the future). Here are some of them:

- Wars.

- Famines (starving people).

- Disease (cancer, AIDS, etc.).

- Earthquakes.

- Heart disease.

- Stress.

- Selfishness.

- Greed.

- Homosexual increase ("gay" people).

- Violence.

- Calls for peace.

Hypocrisy
(fake Christians).

Knowledge.

Remember, all these prophecies were written thousands of years [7] ago. The Bible says that people would laugh and say that these things have always been around. But Jesus warned that the sign to look for was when the Jews got Jerusalem back. That happened in 1967 (after 2,000 years of not having their own homeland).

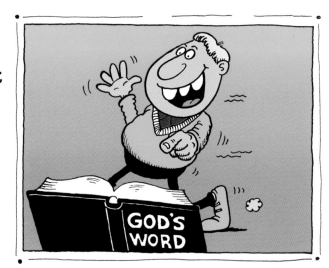

If all these things were written in the Bible (and only God could have known that they would happen), that tells us that the men who wrote the Bible were inspired (helped) by God. If that is the case, everything in it is true because it is impossible for God to [8] lie. You can completely trust it... *including His promise of everlasting [9] life.*

Some people say that the Bible has been changed down through the centuries, but in 1949, some scrolls (rolled up pieces of paper) were found near the Dead Sea in Israel. These were large parts of the Bible that were written thousands of years ago. When they were compared to the modern Bible, they were the same. The Bible hasn't changed in all that time. It is still the world's best-selling book. Hundreds of millions of copies are printed each year and it's been translated into more than 1200 languages.

[1] See 2 Timothy 3:16

[2] See Isaiah 40:22

[3] See Job 26:7

[4] See Hebrews 11:3

[5] See Leviticus 15:13

[6] See Leviticus 17:11

[7] For more "signs" see Matthew 24, Luke 21, 1 Timothy 1:4, 2 Timothy 3, 2 Peter 2:1-3 and Daniel 12:4

[8] See Hebrews 6:18

[9] See John 3:16

[10] See, *The Evidence Bible* (Bridge-Logos).

If you believe God's promises (His Bible) you are in good company. Many famous people believed them--including George Washington, Thomas Jefferson, Teddy Roosevelt, Charles Dickens, Sir Winston Churchill and [10] Abraham Lincoln.

Way back in the 1800's, a man named Charles Darwin had an idea. He thought that perhaps people weren't made by God as the Bible says, but instead came from monkeys. He even wrote a book about his idea. It was called, *Origin of the Species*. It came out in 1859 and sold a lot of copies. Mr. Darwin's idea was called "Darwin's theory (idea) of evolution." The word "evolution" means "change."

If the idea of evolution was right, then the Bible was wrong. The Bible said that God made Adam and Eve... and they were people, *not* monkeys. Many stopped believing the Bible and instead believed that people came from monkeys.

Other men (scientists) thought up more ideas about evolution. They even said that they had found bones that proved that Mr. Darwin was right.

In 1912, someone found a man's skull that looked like it was from a large monkey. This was what had been missing since Mr. Darwin first had his idea-- something that showed that men were once monkeys. It was called "the missing link." It was a big discovery and scientists said that it *proved* the idea of evolution. They called it "Piltdown Man" and said that it was about a million years old. They believed it showed that the Bible was wrong.

Then, in 1953, it was found that it was all a big trick. Piltdown Man's skull was only 600 years old. The jawbone that was with it was 500 years old, and was a big monkey's jaw. [1]

Other scientists discovered "Nebraska Man." This one was made up from one tooth. But it was discovered later that this one was also a trick. It was just the tooth of a dead pig.

There have been many other discoveries of bones that many people thought were proof of Mr. Darwin's idea, but they also turned out to be [2] hoaxes (a trick).

Some people still think that evolution is true. They even make up pictures of monkeys turning into men,

to try and convince people that it did happen. But it can't be [3] proven. Some scientists say that Mr. Darwin's idea is just "a fairy tale for [4] grown-ups" and that those who go around telling people it is true are [5] "con-men" (liars).

It's silly to think that people came from monkeys. The Bible teaches us that every animal "brings forth after its own [6] kind." You can see that that is true everywhere you look. Dogs don't have kittens; they have puppies. Sheep don't have dogs; they have lambs. Pigs have piglets, rabbits have rabbits, fish have fish, and people have people (babies)--not [7] monkeys. After all these years, still no one has found Mr. Darwin's "missing link."

Dr. Kent Hovind has studied evolution closely. He says that he will give $250,000 to anyone who can give proof that the idea is [8] true. No one can do it... because it's not true. However, it is easy to prove that the Bible is [9] true.

[1] *Our Times*--the Illustrated History of the 20th Century (Turner Publishing, 1995, page 94).

[2] See "Evolution" *The Evidence Bible* (Bridge-Logos).

[3] Sir Arthur Keith--he wrote the foreword to the 100th edition of, *Origin of the Species*.

[4] Professor Louis Bounoure, Director of Research, National Center of Scientific Research.

[5] Dr. T. N. Tahmisian, Atomic Energy Commission, USA.

[6] See Genesis 1:24

[7] See 1 Corinthians 15:39

[8] See: www.drdino.com/Articles/Article1.htm

Do you ever wonder why **God** lets bad things happen to people? They get sick. There are terrible earthquakes, floods, tornadoes and hurricanes. The Bible says that when **God** made

Adam and **Eve**, everything was wonderful. When they sinned, these **bad** things came with it.

But God promises that a new world is coming (God's Kingdom), and all those who truly love Him will get new bodies that will never have pain or tears. We show that we love God by obeying what He says in the Bible. (Romans 5:12, Romans 8:20-23, 1 Corinthians 15:42-58, Philippians 3:21, 2 Peter 3:13).

Here's a good question.
Who made God?
Here's a good answer. *Nobody*.
He didn't have a beginning.
That sounds strange to us
because we live in "time." God lives
in "eternity," where there is no
time. He just is. It's hard to figure
out, but it's true. (Psalm 90:2,
Revelation 10:6).

Now we are going
to test your memory
to see if you
are a genius!

TEST NUMBER ONE

Memorize the **Ten Commandments** using these special picture figures. Then test your memory, and grade yourself.

Put each picture in your mind, and it will remind you of each commandment.

1. **"You shall have no other gods before Me"**
(God should be Number One)

2. **"You shall not make yourself any graven image"**
(Don't bow down to anything but God)

3. "You shall not take the name of the Lord your God in vain"

(Don't use your lips to dishonor God)

4. "Remember the Sabbath Day to keep it holy"

(Don't neglect the things of God)

5. "Honor your Father and your Mother"

6. "You shall not kill"

7. "You shall not commit adultery"
(Adultery leaves a heart broken)

8. "You shall not steal"

9. "You shall not lie"
(a "lying" nine)

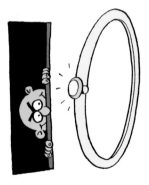

10. "You shall not covet"
(want what others have)

Now, get a pen...

...and check your memory

What is number...

10 _____

_____

9 _____

_____

8 _____

_____

7 _____

_____

6 _____

_____

and what is number...

5 _____
_____

4 _____
_____

3 _____
_____

2 _____
_____

1 _____
_____

**If you remembered five you did O.K....
but you need to try again.**

Six... you did well.

Seven... good.

Eight... very good.

Nine... wonderful!

Ten... you're a **Genius!**

Why do you think that God gave us the Ten Commandments?

A As a way to get to Heaven?

B As a mirror to look at?

If you chose "A" you are

~~rong~~

~~wronge~~

wrong

57

In the same way, we don't realize what a bad state we are in until we look into the "mirror" of the Ten Commandments.

Do you remember number 9?
What is it?
Have you ever lied?

What about number 5?
Have you always obeyed your parents?

How about number 6?
The Bible says if you hate someone,
you've committed murder.

Have you always loved God?

Have you ever stolen something?

Have you ever been greedy?

Can you see that the **Ten Commandments** are like the mirror --
they show us how bad we are,
and how we need to be clean before the **Day of Judgment.**

That is the **Day God** will punish people who have broken the **Ten Commandments.**

They will be sent to a place called "Hell"- a place where God doesn't want people to go.

God doesn't want you to be punished.

He so loves you that He made a way for you to be clean before Judgment Day

To show you what a wonderful thing God did, listen to this story.

A man had a son who was really bad. He did many bad things, including lying and stealing, and found himself in trouble with the police.

THE LONG ARM OF THE LAW

They said he had to pay a $50,000 fine or go to prison. The son didn't have any money, and was about to go to prison.

Then his **dad** stepped in and used his life savings to pay his son's fine. That meant that he **didn't** have to go to prison.

It showed how much he loved his son.

We are like that son.

But God came down to earth and paid our fine by dying on the Cross.

Jesus took our punishment on Himself.

Then He rose from the dead.

That means that we don't have to be punished by God. We can live with Him forever!

It also shows us how much God loves us.

What should you do?

Ask God to forgive you
for the Commandments you've broken
(this is called "sin"),
and then give your life to Jesus.

Read Psalm 51 and make it your own prayer.
When you do that, you will have God's promise
that you are forgiven and will live forever.

Then read your Bible every day
(it's full of incredible stories --
start with the Gospel of John),
and obey what you read.

God will never leave you.

Don't Miss:
The Evidence Bible
—for parents

Irrefutable evidence *for the thinking mind...*

Learn how to show the absurdity of evolution.
Study how to share your faith with your family or at your workplace.
Learn how to witness to an atheist.
See from scripture how to prove God's existence without the use of faith.
Discover how to prove the authenticity of the Bible through prophecy.
See how the Bible is full of eye-opening scientific and medical facts.
Read fascinating quotes from Charles Darwin, Albert Einstein, Sir Isaac Newton, Louis Pasteur,
Stephen Hawking, many other well-known scientists.
Read the fearful last words of famous people who died without the Savior.
Learn how to refute the "contradictions" in the Bible.
Read incredible quotes about the Bible from presidents and other famous people.
Discover how to answer questions such as Where did Cain get his wife? Why there is suffering.
Why the dinosaur disappeared...and much more.